DATE			

CUP

© THE BAKER & TAYLOR CO.

ELEPHANTS ON THE BEACH

ELEPHANTS
ON THE
BEACH

Irene Brady

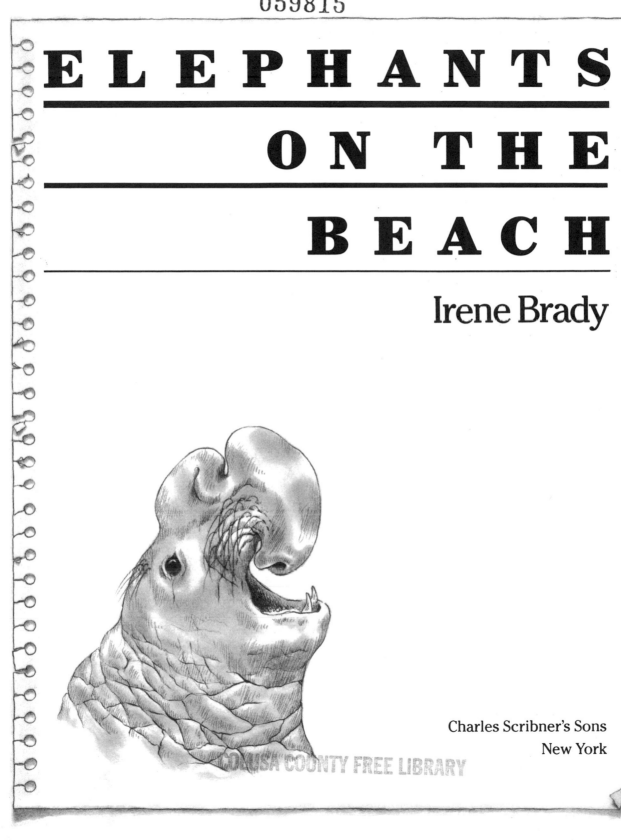

Charles Scribner's Sons
New York

Copyright © 1979, 1978 Irene Brady

Library of Congress Cataloging in Publication Data
Brady, Irene.
  Elephants on the beach.
  SUMMARY: Describes the physical characteristics and
habits of the northern elephant seal.
  1. Northern elephant seal — Juvenile literature.
[1. Northern elephant seal. 2. Seals (Animals)]
I. Title.
QL737.P64B72   599'.748   79-89
ISBN 0-684-16115-X

"Elephants on the Beach" appeared in slightly
different form in the March, 1978 issue of *Audubon*.

1 3 5 7 9 11 13 15 17 19   RD/C   20 18 16 14 12 10 8 6 4 2

Printed in the United States of America

for David

March 15, 8:50 a.m.
It's a good day for a sketching trip.
Warm sunshine, a cool breeze and a beautiful, lonely California
beach.. Willets glide past the dunes. Maybe a sandpiper
made these tracks.

Gumboot chiton

It looks as if no one ever comes here to carry away shells or trample the windrows of seaweed. I've found twelve kinds of seaweed within reach without moving.

A ring-billed gull is watching me from only four meters away.

The beach is covered with tiny abalone shells, sea urchin tests, wavy turbans, crabs, and big gumboot chitons (Giant Pacific Chitons).

This gumboot chiton was twenty-eight centimeters long (or 8½EEE as gumboots might be measured) and was a bright pinkish orange with freckles.

The gulls drift and wheel over the surf. I could watch them all day.

some quick gull sketches (ring-billed gull)

10:10 AM. Too bad!—a beautiful silvery seal dead on the beach. I can't see any blood or injury, but it's lying with its head under water and isn't breathi— uh...there's something strange going on here!

I was squatting in cold, salty water for ten minutes sketching this seal between waves, and I <u>know</u> it didn't breathe in all that time.

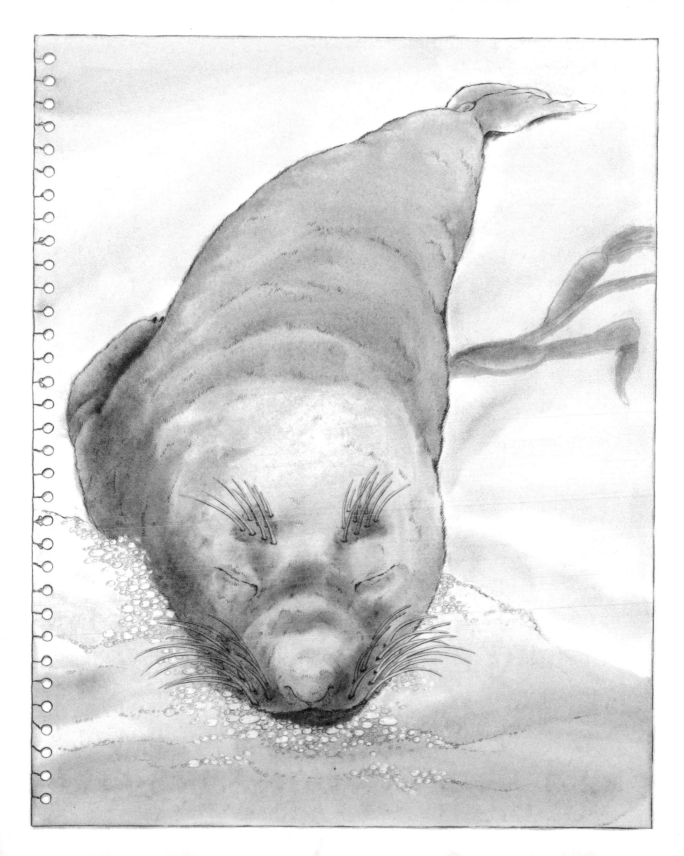

Suddenly it lifted its head out of the water, opened its nostrils from closed slits to round holes, and breathed noisily forty-eight times, eyes still shut.

And now it has "died" again with its head under water! Oh boy—was I ever fooled!

I can't figure this seal out. It's the right size for a harbor seal, but harbor seals are spotted. Sea lions and fur seals live around here, but they have brown pelts and long, thin ears.

What is it?

sea lions and fur seals
have ears like this.

this calf is slightly over one meter long, velvety black in an oversized fur coat which wrinkles when it turns its head or moves. It still has its stump of an umbilical cord attached, so it must be only a day or two old.

this other calf is at least twice as big as the black one and has silver fur — AHA! this explains my mystery seal down the beach.

the silver calves must be several weeks older than the black calf since the black coat is molted and replaced by a silver coat at about 5 weeks.

10:30 AM. WOW! What a shock! When I started over the next dune, I almost ran into a huge, wrinkled bull elephant seal, basking on the sandy beach with his harem of three cows and two calves.

I'm lying out flat on the sand, trying to keep out of sight behind this dune.

The bull is about four meters long and a meter high. The cows are only about one-third his size (and <u>much</u> prettier).

I know the Southern Elephant Seal stays south of California, so these must be Northern Elephant Seals. They usually stay on offshore islands to escape people. I'm lucky to find them here.

I'd like to get closer to sketch, but I've read that they move pretty fast, and this bull doesn't look very friendly. Also, I don't want to scare them away from this beach.

The binoculars help a lot.

this is the silver calf

Belly

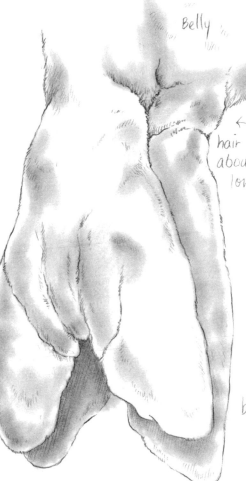

hair is about 1/8" long

back flippers on silver calf

left front flipper

11:40 AM. The bull suddenly noticed me and reared up with a roar—I can't quite describe it (blood-curdling? bone-chilling?). Sort of a loud, honking bellow, anyway. Then he started to lurch toward me (I'm crouched behind a dune with only my head showing, about ten meters away from the harem).

But then he stopped and forgot about me, I guess, because he went back to his harem. Maybe he figured he'd scared me enough. He did, too.

I think I'll try to sneak to a spot about seven meters above the harem where they can't see me as well.

2:05 PM. This new place is much better. I've been sketching here for almost two hours. The black turnstones have come back again, and the herring gulls and ring-billed gulls, too, doing what shorebirds do—skittering up and down with the waves. They don't pay any attention to the elephant seals, and the seals ignore them, too. The seals are very sluggish. I can move and make little noises, and they don't seem to notice.

I'm hidden behind a dune, all but my head, looking through a willow bush.

the skin here is very thick with deep cracks.
nostril
this herring gull really has nerve!

black turnstones

the smallest calf has wiggled close to a
female's belly (its mother?) and is nursing.

2:20 PM. Every once in a while the bull grunts, opens an eye, and flips sand up on his body. I don't know why—maybe to keep cool or keep flies or parasites away? Perhaps to keep his skin damp? He's almost covered with sand now, and there's a big hole in the sand next to him which he has scraped out with his flipper. The calves and females are all flipping sand, too.

They're a lot more agile than they look. They can scratch almost every part of their bodies if they really try.

One of the cows is restless...off to sea! She moves like an inchworm. First she arches her back and plants her rear flippers firmly in the sand. Then she shoves her front end forward with a lurch. And then she arches her back again and keeps right on going. In a way, she's almost graceful. She's going about as fast as I could walk.

I wish I could see her underwater. I've heard they swim very gracefully.

there's a brush rabbit about three meters from me in a clump of lupine munching some greens. It seems curious about me, but too wary to come much close

Notes from the next day, March 16.
I wouldn't have believed an animal as big as that bull elephant seal could move so quietly.

Sketching the brush rabbit, I forgot the giants just over the dune. The bull got within five meters of me (I <u>didn't</u> stop to measure it!) on his way into the dunes for an afternoon snooze.

I scrambled out of there as fast as I could (and not as gracefully as an elephant seal, either). I was in such a hurry that I left my sketch pad behind. It ended up right under his snoring nose, and I couldn't get it back until he woke up and lumbered back to his harem five hours later.

But I'm not complaining.

It really was a good day
for a sketching trip.